STEAM ACROSS THE PENNINES

Anthony Dawson

AMBERLEY

First published 2018

Amberley Publishing
The Hill, Stroud
Gloucestershire, GL5 4EP

www.amberley-books.com

Copyright © Anthony Dawson, 2018

The right of Anthony Dawson to be identified
as the Author of this work has been asserted in
accordance with the Copyrights, Designs and
Patents Act 1988.

ISBN 978 1 4456 7096 6 (print)
ISBN 978 1 4456 7097 3 (ebook)

British Library Cataloguing in Publication Data.
A catalogue record for this book is available from
the British Library.

Origination by Amberley Publishing.
Printed in the UK.

Introduction

The Pennines, the 'backbone of England', run for 267 miles from Edale in the Derbyshire Peaks almost due north to the Tyne Gap, forming a natural barrier between the ancient rivals of Yorkshire and Lancashire. They first presented an engineering challenge to the Romans in their conquest of the North (AD 44–80) as they built their network of roads and forts. Then the turnpike and canal builders of the eighteenth and nineteenth centuries. In fact, the Pennines presented such a problem to the builders of the Liverpool & Leeds Canal (which took fifty years to complete) that they tried their best to avoid them. A similar approach taken by George Stephenson, engineer of the Manchester & Leeds Railways – the first trans-Pennine railway – which meanders through the Calder Valley in order to avoid the worst of the Pennine chain, but was forced to dig what was then Britain's longest tunnel at Littleborough (1.6 miles). The first section from Manchester Oldham Road to Littleborough opened on 3 July 1839, and the whole route through to Leeds in 1841.

Success of Stephenson's railway inspired other main lines through the Pennines. The first was the Woodhead Route, which was conceived to link Sheffield with Manchester via the Longdendale Valley. Originally engineered by Stephenson's great rival, Charles Blacker Vignoles, it necessitated the digging of the first of three tunnels at Woodhead, during which thirty-two men were killed and 140 seriously wounded, 'besides the sick'. Social reformer Edwin Chadwick stated that the Woodhead Tunnel had a higher casualty rate than one of Wellington's battles in the Peninsular War. Work started in 1838 but Vignoles was dismissed a year later to be replaced by George Stephenson's great protégé, Joseph Locke. After seven years of work, the line opened in 1845, and almost immediately a second tunnel at Woodhead was needed; thus, Woodhead 2 opened in 1852. The Woodhead Route was electrified between 1939 and 1953, which also saw the construction of a third tunnel (Woodhead 3, in 1953). It was controversially closed in 1981.

Thus, by the 1840s there were two main line railways crossing the Pennines, but neither provided a direct route between 'Cottonopolis' (Manchester) and the textile (and later engineering) centre of Leeds. A third main line, via Huddersfield, was proposed as early as 1835 but it took nearly ten years before it got off the ground and was eventually constructed by two different companies: the Huddersfield & Manchester Railway & Canal Company and the Leeds, Dewsbury & Manchester Railway Company. The Huddersfield line was surveyed by Locke, and his route required considerable tunnelling at Standedge and Morley; the section of line between Stalybridge and Huddersfield mirrored that of the existing Huddersfield Narrow Canal of 1811. Both companies built a grand station at Huddersfield – described by Sir John Betjeman as one of the finest in England. In fact, Henry Booth, the secretary of the LNWR, thought it perhaps too grand and future generations are lucky that his proposal to demolish half of it was never acted upon.

George Stephenson was busy in Yorkshire during the 1840s; he was the engineer to the Leeds & Bradford Railway, which ran from Leeds Wellington station (now demolished) through Airedale to Bradford Forster Square, opening with a somewhat farcical ceremony in 1846. Even before the L&B had opened various 'extension' companies were proposed, pushing the line further west into the hills. The Leeds & Bradford Extension Railway of 1845 opened from Shipley through to Colne, with the first section to be opened being between Bradford and Shipley, where there was a triangular junction where a branch to Keighley diverged. Onward travel down the Worth Valley to Oxenhope would have to wait another twenty years, however, until 1867, when the Worth Valley Railway, engineered by John McLandsborough, was opened – though the final opening was delayed due, it is said, to a cow eating the engineers' plans! The tunnel under Halifax Road at Ingrow caused substantial damage to the recently completed Wesleyan chapel, and after arbitration the railway company had to pay for a new building on a slightly different site. The Great Northern Railway's Queensbury line, which had its own station at Ingrow, was opened in 1884 and closed in 1955. The Worth Valley line was threatened with closure in 1959, but strong local opposition forestalled this proposal until 1961. It took the preservation society eight frustrating years before they could run trains.

Growing out of the great 'Railway Mania' of the mid-1840s was the embryonic East Lancashire Railway, which grew from a tangled web of lines in East Lancashire promoted by local businessmen. What is now the preserved East Lancashire Railway (from Bury Bolton Street to Rawtenstall) received its Act in 1844. The Blackburn and Preston line had the almost ubiquitous Joseph Locke as engineer, while the line to Rossendale was engineered by another Stephenson alumnus, Thomas Gooch. Finally, the Blackburn, Burnley, Accrington & Colne Extension Railway proposed an end-on junction at Colne (where it met the Leeds & Bradford Extension Railway), providing a trans-Pennine route to Leeds via Skipton. An Act of Parliament of July 1845 incorporated these diverse schemes as the East Lancashire Railway. The 11½-mile Skipton–Colne link closed in 1970 but Transport for the North and Lancashire County Council are supportive (as of spring 2018) of its re-opening, with the Department of Transport cooperating on a feasibility study.

Skipton soon became a major railway centre and was the heart of the Little North Western Railway (incorporated in 1846, part of the Midland from 1852), which was to build a railway from Skipton to a junction on the Lancaster & Carlisle Railway, 4½ miles south of Tebay, as well as a branch through to Lancaster. This provided the Midland Railway with its own route to Scotland, rivalling that of the mighty London & North Western Railway.

So fierce was this rivalry that one of the most spectacular railways in Britain was the result: the 73-mile Settle & Carlisle. Construction began in 1869, with over 6,000 navvies labouring in harsh conditions for six years. One of the navvy camps was the subject of an archaeological dig by *Time Team*. Even with modern gortex and a catering truck it was cold and miserable for the archaeologists, but it would have been even more so for the navvies – like 'Big Rachel' – in the 1870s.

Skipton was also the focus of a much less ambitious scheme, but one which grew out of an equal rivalry. The Wharfedale Railway had originally been proposed in 1852, but it wasn't until the mid-1860s that the Otley & Ilkley Joint Railway, engineered by John McLandsborough, was operated by the North Eastern & Midland Railway, opening as far as Ilkley in 1865. The onward extension through upper Wharfedale to Skipton was opened in 1888, but fell victim to Beeching's infamous cuts in 1965. Fortunately, the section from Embsay to the beauty spot of Bolton Abbey is now home to the Embsay & Bolton Abbey Steam Railway.

The final trans-Pennine route was to link the Midland Railway at Hawes on the Settle & Carlisle to the North Eastern at Northallerton via Wensleydale. Various schemes were proposed during the 'Railway Mania' of the 1840s, but the route which finally emerged was opened in stages from the 1860s to 1878. Naturally enough for an area renowned for its dairy produce, the mainstay of traffic was milk: by the turn of the twentieth century, more than 10,000 gallons of milk per week were being carried on the Wensleydale Railway, and both the Midland and North Eastern encouraged milk traffic on the line, supporting the construction of dairies close to the Redmire and Northallerton stations. The Wensleydale Railway was an early victim of railway closures, with passenger services being withdrawn as early as 1954 and the section from Hawes to Redmire closing in 1959, while the remaining section was used for stone and MoD traffic until 1992. Coming to the rescue was the Wensleydale Railway Association (formed in 1990), which in 2003 obtained a ninety-nine-year lease on the Wensleydale Railway with the ultimate aim of re-opening the entire route. As a result, closed stations were re-opened and a new station was built at Northallerton West.

Under the BR Modernisation Plan, steam was withdrawn on many trans-Pennine services, to be replaced by first-generation DMUs. However, steam was still very much to the fore for long-distance and especially freight workings until its final demise in 1968.

After this, the only place to see steam was on preserved lines, including the pioneering Middleton Railway (1959) or the Worth Valley, which re-opened after many years of frustration in 1968 and which won international fame as the location for the classic *The Railway Children* of 1970. The Worth Valley is unique in preserving a branch line in its entirety. The Embsay & Bolton re-opened a short section in 1979 (after a few false starts), finally reaching Bolton Abbey in 1998. It carries 10,000 passengers per year. The Kirklees Light Railway began running its 15-inch gauge trains in 1991 along part of the defunct Clayton West Branch, while the East Lancashire Railway began running trains in 1987.

BR's ban on main line steam was lifted after only three years in 1971. The Steam Locomotive Operators' Association was formed in 1975 and was able to better negotiate with BR to organise main line steam tours. Perhaps one of the most famous of these was the 'Scarborough Spa Express' from York to Scarborough, which first ran from 1981 to 1988, recommencing in 2002 with a circular route via Harrogate and Leeds, or the 'Tin Bath Special.' During 2018 there were several popular steam charters running through the Pennines, including the 'Scarborough Spa' (Carnforth–Skipton–York–Scarborough); 'The Dalesman' (York–Carlisle); 'The Waverley' (York–Leeds–Settle-Carlisle) and 'The East Yorkshireman' (Manchester–Scarborough).

Although steam officially ended in the Pennines in 1968, fifty years later it is alive and well thanks to pioneering efforts at the Middleton Railway. Preserved railways such as the East Lancashire Railway and Worth Valley carry over 100,000 passengers per year, with the East Lancashire having an annual turnover of £1.4 million. Steam is big business and preserved lines are major players in the tourist industry, ploughing money back into the local economy. Nationally, preserved steam railways generate around £250 million per year. Steam is certainly alive and well across the Pennines.

The Manchester & Leeds was the first trans-Pennine railway, opening despite much opposition in July 1839. Here we see Hebden Bridge in 1844. (Anthony Dawson Collection)

George Stephenson's viaduct has dominated Todmorden for 180 years; it is seen here in 1844. (Anthony Dawson Collection)

Brighouse station on the Manchester & Leeds, drawn by A. F. Tait in 1844. (Anthony Dawson Collection)

Wakefield's first station was built near Kirkgate, on what had formerly been strawberry fields and Joseph Aspdin's Portland Cement Works. (Anthony Dawson Collection)

The brooding portal of Summit Tunnel; when it opened in 1841 it was the world's longest railway tunnel. (Anthony Dawson Collection)

A magnificent stone building replaced the original timber structure at Wakefield Kirkgate in 1854. (Anthony Dawson Collection)

Victoria was built by Fairbairn of Manchester to a design of Edward Bury for the Manchester, Bolton & Bury Railway in the 1840s. (Anthony Dawson Collection)

The Bury type was the mainstay of Manchester & Leeds and early Lancashire & Yorkshire motive power. (Anthony Dawson Collection)

Radial Tank No. 696 was designed by Aspinall and built at Horwich in August 1898. Seen here at Wakefield Kirkgate in 1908, she was scrapped forty-seven years later in 1947. (Anthony Dawson Collection)

One of Aspinall's 1220 Class 4-4-0s. No. 488 of April 1894 was photographed at Leeds in July 1905; she was withdrawn in March 1917. (Anthony Dawson)

Radial Tank No. 1349 (built March 1897) is seen on the turntable at Leeds on 9 June 1906. (Anthony Dawson)

Another one of Aspinall's Radial Tanks, No. 1348 of March 1897 is seen at Leeds waiting for the right away in summer 1905. (Anthony Dawson Collection)

Built by Hoy in 1902, No. 632 was fitted with experimental Druitt Halpin thermal storage apparatus (the large drum on top of the boiler barrel). She was photographed at Leeds in summer 1905. (Anthony Dawson Collection)

Built by Beyer, Peacock of Gorton, L&YR 4-4-0 No. 988 poses for the camera at Leeds in 1905. (Anthony Dawson Collection)

Holbeck Locomotive Depot opened in 1868 as Midland Shed No. 28, latterly 20A and 50A under BR. Black Five No. 45597 stands in the yard in 1961. (Anthony Dawson Collection)

A work-worn A3 Pacific, No. 60070 *Gladiateur* (built by North British in 1924) is seen at Holbeck Loco in 1961. (Anthony Dawson Collection)

BR Standard 3MT No. 77012 is seen at Holbeck Loco on 7 September 1961. One of a class of only twenty, she was scrapped in 1967. (Anthony Dawson Collection)

Filthy Black Five No. 45219 is seen 'in the yard at Holbeck Loco [in] 1966'. She was withdrawn a year later and scrapped in 1968. (Anthony Dawson Collection)

Bulleid Pacific No. 34051 *Winston Churchill* makes a curious sight at Holbeck in December 1965. (Anthony Dawson Collection)

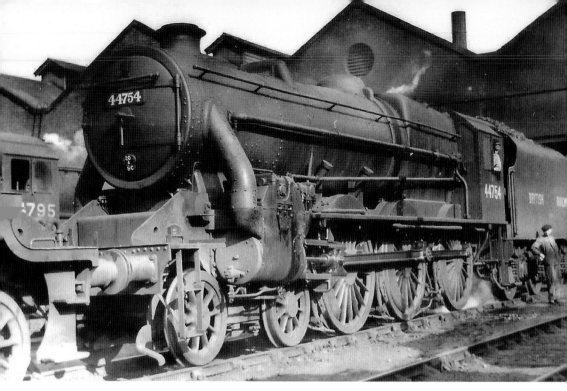

A brand-new Caprotti valve-gear-fitted Black Five, No. 44754 stands outside Holbeck Loco in 1948. She was scrapped in 1964. (Anthony Dawson Collection)

Neville Hill shed was opened by the North Eastern Railway in 1901; its smoky interior is seen here on 5 June 1966. (Anthony Dawson Collection)

Neville Hill Roundhouse on 13 May 1963, with a mix of ex-LNER and BR motive power present. (Anthony Dawson Collection)

Ex-LNER Thompson B1 No. 61259 heads west with a rake of Gresley coaches on 19 April 1954. (Anthony Dawson Collection)

Former LMS Royal Scot No. 46133 *The Green Howards* departs Leeds City in 1948. (Anthony Dawson Collection)

Ex-LNER A3 Pacific No. 60018 *Gay Crusader* heads the Up 'White Rose' from Leeds Central. (Anthony Dawson Collection)

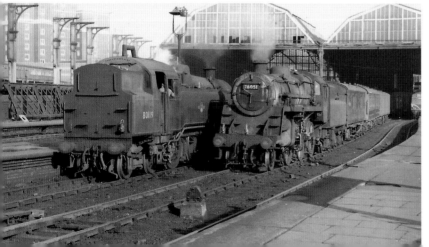

Leeds City in the 1960s was in a period of transition: filthy steam engines (both less than a decade old) and an immaculate first-generation DMU present quite a contrast in September 1961. (Anthony Dawson Collection)

Above and below: Described as one of the finest railway stations in the country, Huddersfield was opened by the Leeds, Dewsbury & Manchester and Huddersfield & Manchester Railway & Canal Company *c.* 1846–50. It is seen here in LNWR and LMS days. (Anthony Dawson Collection)

L. M. S. Railway Station, Huddersfield.

Former LNWR Prince of Wales Class No. 5712 is seen in LMS days as it heads into Huddersfield. (Anthony Dawson Collection)

Fowler 4P No. 12375 is seen at Luddenfoot with a mixed bag of Midland Railway carriages in the early 1930s. (Anthony Dawson Collection)

Hughes Crab No. 2711 (built at Horwich in March 1927) is also at Luddendenfoot, with a more up-to-date rake of carriages. (Anthony Dawson Collection)

Royal Scot No. 6118 *Royal Welch Fusilier* is seen 'near Huddersfield' in the 1930s. (Anthony Dawson Collection)

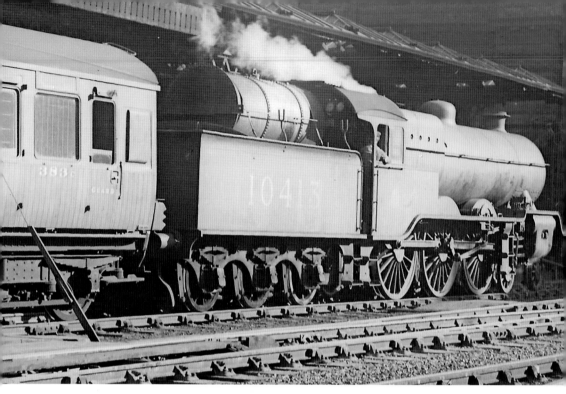

Ex-LYR N1 class (of March 1909) in LMS days as No. 10413, and converted as an oil burner, standing at Platform 3 at Bradford Exchange with the 5 p.m. departure for Marylebone in 1926. (Anthony Dawson Collection)

A busy day at Skipton on 30 June 1935. (Anthony Dawson Collection)

The 'Thames Clyde Express' clatters through Skipton, headed by A3 Pacific No. 60080 *Dick Turpin c.* 1960. (Anthony Dawson Collection)

Manchester, Sheffield & Lincolnshire Railway No. 404 is seen standing at Sheffield Victoria, *c.* 1870. (Anthony Dawson Collection)

Penistone Junction *c.* 1900, where the L&YR branch from Huddersfield met the Great Central main line to Sheffield. (Anthony Dawson Collection)

A Robinson 2-8-0 heavy freight locomotive, No. 2318 clanks its way to Sheffield on the Woodhead Route in May 1928. (Anthony Dawson Collection)

Electric replaces steam at Sheffield Victoria: BR Standard No. 73069 is released as EM2 No. 27003 *Diana* couples up to take the train forward to Manchester. (Anthony Dawson Collection)

Before BR steam officially ended there was a spree of main line specials, including this one organised by the Locomotive Club of Great Britain. LMS Jubilee No. 45593 *Kohlapur* stands in the pouring rain at Ribblehead. (Anthony Dawson Collection)

That's yer lot! IT57 (the 'Fifteen Guinea Special') ran through the Pennines from Liverpool to Manchester and Carlisle and back on 11 August 1968. (Anthony Dawson Collection)

Above and below: Early days at the Middleton with scrubbed-up coal wagons and brake van rides. (Anthony Dawson Collection)

The recently restored *Brookes No. 1* (Hunslet works number 2387 of 1941) simmers at Moor Road station in the winter of 2017. (Ian Hardman)

Having passed under the M1, *Brookes No. 1* approaches the points for the Dartmouth Branch. (Ian Hardman)

The immaculate cab of *Brookes No. 1*, the driver having left a billy of tea to warm. (Ian Hardman)

Driver's eye view of Moor Road. (Ian Hardman)

Brookes No. 1 bursts through the short tunnel under the M1 motorway. (Ian Hardman)

And approaches the Middleton Park Halt terminus on a winter's afternoon in 2017. (Ian Hardman)

Brookes No. 1 departs Moor Road. (Ian Hardman)

Returning down-grade from Middleton Park Halt. (Ian Hardman)

The urban character of the Middleton Railway is clear as *Brookes No. 1* heads away from Moor Road. (Ian Hardman)

Standing at Middleton Park Halt, about to run round. (Ian Hardman)

The Middleton Railway has always had a locomotive named *Matthew Murray* after the Leeds-based engineer. Manning Wardle 'L Class' (works number 1601 of 1903) takes water at Moor Road. (Ian Hardman)

Vertical-boilered Sentinel No. 68153 has been a mainstay of the Middleton for decades: she is seen here in pristine condition in the 'Engine House' museum following restoration to working order. (Ian Hardman)

Matthew Murray makes a spirited run to Middleton Park Halt. (Ian Hardman)

The end of the line – for now? *Matthew Murray* stands at the blocks at Middleton Park Halt. An extension into Middleton Park has been planned for several years. (Ian Hardman)

The last passenger train run on the Worth Valley was a special charter on 23 June 1962 headed by former Midland 3F No. 43856. (Anthony Dawson Collection)

The tunnel at Ingrow, which caused so many problems when building the line. The now closed Wesleyan chapel (which partially collapsed) is visible top left. (Anthony Dawson)

Early preservation days at Howarth: USATC S100 No. 30072 turned out in an attractive ochre 'house livery' and Ivatt tank no. 41241 in crimson lake. Both worked the re-opening special on 29 June 1968. (Anthony Dawson Collection)

Ex-GWR 57XX Pannier Tank No. 5775 is seen at Howarth in London Transport colours, to whom it was sold in 1963. She starred in the EMI film *The Railway Children* (1970) painted in the fictitious livery of the Great Northern & Southern Railway. (Anthony Dawson Collection)

USATC S160 'Big Jim' No. 5820, shortly after arrival in Yorkshire from Poland in 1977. (Anthony Dawson Collection)

Longmoor Military Railway No. 118 *Brussels* heads a short passenger train in January 1977. (Anthony Dawson Collection)

Former Longmoor Military Railway No. 118 *Brussels* heads a short passenger train in January 1977. (Anthony Dawson Collection)

Former Midland 4F No. 43924 powers round the curve from Keighley. (Ian Hardman)

Midland super power: Fowler 7F No. 53808, built for the steeply-graded Somerset & Dorset in 1925, is looking at home at Keighley. (Ian Hardman)

LMS Black Five No. 44871, which famously worked one leg of the 'Fifteen Guinea Special' in August 1968. (Ian Hardman)

Visiting LNER Thompson B1 Class No. 61264 is seen running light engine at Keighley. (Ian Hardman)

Main line-certified Black Five No. 45212 also had the distinction of working the last revenue-earning main line steam service on BR. (Ian Hardman)

Owned by the Bahamas Locomotive Society, *Nunlow* (built by Hudswell Clarke & Co. as works number 1708 in 1938) is seen waiting for the right away at Keighley. (Ian Hardman)

Victorian engines united: Beattie Well Tank No. 30587 made a visit to its home town of Manchester (the first time since she was built in 1874!) in summer 2017 and also visited Keighley. She is seen in the company of LNWR Coal Tank No. 1054. (Ian Hardman)

An immaculately turned out Webb Coal Tank simmers at Oxenhope. (Ian Hardman)

No. 30587 stands in the yard at Ingrow while Taff Vale Railway 01 Class tank No. 28 runs past toward Keighley. (Ian Hardman)

Old and new: over fifty years separate Taff Vale Tank No. 28 (built by Kitson & Co. in 1894) and War Department Austerity No. 90733 (built by Vulcan in 1945). (Ian Hardman)

No. 30587 waiting for the off from Ingrow to Keighley. (Ian Hardman)

Victorian tanks meet: a volcano-like Taff Vale Tank rounds the curve into Ingrow. (Ian Hardman)

No. 90733 stands on shed at Howarth. She was repatriated from Sweden in 1973 and was restored to British condition between 1993 and 2007. (Ian Hardman)

Resplendent in LMS crimson lake, Hughes Crab No. 13065. She returned to service following a lengthy overhaul in 2014. (Ian Hardman)

'Fifteen Guinea Special' survivor No. 70013 *Oliver Cromwell* climbs away from Keighley. (Ian Hardman)

With safety valves lifting, *Oliver Cromwell* impatiently awaits the right away from Keighley. (Ian Hardman)

No. 43924 is seen at sunset at Oxenhope at Christmas 2016. (Anthony Dawson)

Above and below: Now a familiar sight on the East Lancs, Bulleid Pacific *City of Wells* draws her seasonal train into a rather damp Bury Bolton Street. (Ian Hardman)

Main line-registered BR Standard 4 No. 76084 rumbles through Bolton Street. She was restored to steam in 2013. (Ian Hardman)

No. 76084 comes off shed and pulls into Bolton Street. (Ian Hardman)

Black Five No. 44871 arrives on Platform 1 at the lovingly restored Bolton Street station. (Ian Hardman)

The East Lancs often plays host to visiting engines; in this case, Hunslet Engine Co. works no. 2705 *Beatrice* from the Embsay & Bolton Abbey Steam Railway is seen with a dining train. (Ian Hardman)

Another Embsay visitor, GWR 56XX Class tank No. 5643 stands at a wintry Bolton Street. (Ian Hardman)

LNER A4 Pacific No. 6009 *Union of South Africa* starred at the 2017 October Gala, where she made her farewell appearance. (Ian Hardman)

Another farewell, LNER K4 No. 61994 *The Great Marquess* made a visit to Lancashire before being withdrawn by her owner, John Cameron. (Ian Hardman)

8F No. 48624 from the Great Central Railway drifts into Bolton Street. (Ian Hardman)

Above and below: The 'People's Engine': following an extensive (and expensive) overhaul by Ian Riley & Sons, LNER A3 Pacific 60103 *Flying Scotsman* made her first moves under steam at Bury in January 2016. (Ian Hardman)

Engine crew and guard converse at Bolton Street. (Ian Hardman)

City of Wells on shed at Buckley Wells. (Ian Hardman)

Frost glistens as LMS Crab No. 13065 powers over the bridge nears Burrs Country Park. (Ian Hardman)

City of Wells, resplendent with 'Golden Arrow' regalia, makes a spirited run near Burrs. (Ian Hardman)

On more mundane duties, *City of Wells* is seen with a train of restored Southern Railway parcel vans. (Ian Hardman)

The driver and fireman of Black Five No. 45212 keep a good look out as she powers round the curve. (Ian Hardman)

Cows graze as Crab No. 13065 runs past on a lazy summer's day. (Ian Hardman)

Lancashire & Yorkshire Railway 24 Class No. 52322 heads away from Ramsbottom. (Ian Hardman)

Main line power: *City of Wells* meets 8F No. 44871 at Ramsbottom. (Ian Hardman)

No. 76084 makes a fine sight working over Brooksbottom Viaduct near Summerseat. (Ian Hardman)

Black Five No. 45212 is seen in a time warp 1960s moment at the Rawtenstall. (Ian Hardman)

No. 76084 powers over the 'Ski Jump' at Broadfield, which carries the ELR over the Metrolink. (Ian Hardman)

No. 45212 simmers under the late winter sun at Rawtenstall. (Ian Hardman)

Beatrice arrives at Embsay station from Bolton Abbey… (Ian Hardman)

…And runs round, ready to return to the well-known beauty-spot. (Ian Hardman)

Beatrice pauses for the signal at Embsay. (Ian Hardman)

The summer sun beats down as *Beatrice* passes Stoneacre Loop. (Ian Hardman)

Taff Vale Tank No. 85 passes a wintry Holywell Halt with a Santa Special. (Ian Hardman)

Wharfedale echoes with the twin exhausts of No. 85 and Austerity No. 35 *Norman*. (Ian Hardman)

Steel, steam, snow and Santa in Wharfedale. (Ian Hardman)

Smoke erupts from Taff Vale Tank No. 85 as she powers through Stoneacre. (Ian Hardman)

Norman powers through the snow. (Ian Hardman)

Norman and No. 85 rest, side by side at Bolton Abbey Signal Box. (Ian Hardman)

Norman takes on water at Bolton Abbey. (Ian Hardman)

No. 85 takes her turn under the water crane. (Ian Hardman)

'Beware of the Trains': end of the line at Bolton Abbey. (Ian Hardman)

Norman's exhaust hangs in the wintry air as she runs round. (Ian Hardman)

LMS Jubilee No. 45690 *Leander* heads the 'Fellsman' through Bamber Bridge towards Carlisle during summer 2017. (Ian Hardman)

Leander crosses the River Calder over the Whalley Viaduct during summer 2017. (Ian Hardman)

No. 45690 *Leander* on the return leg of the 'Fellsman' tour, re-crossing the Calder. (Ian Hardman)

Black Five No. 44871 and Jubilee No. 45699 meet vintage traction at Romiley on 14 February 2016. (Ian Hardman)

No. 45699 *Galatea* exits Wilpshire Tunnel while working the return leg of the 'Fellsman' on 29 May 2018. (Ian Hardman)

The 'Tin Bath Special' passes Romiley, bound for Sheffield on Valentine's Day 2016. (Ian Hardman)

A pair of Black Fives – Nos 44871 and 45407 *The Lancashire Fusilier* – arrive at Manchester Victoria with the 'Tin Bath'. (Ian Hardman)

No. 44871 leads No. 45407 past Crow's Nest, heading for Sheffield on 6 November 2016. (Ian Hardman)

Standard 4 No. 76084 pilots No. 45690 through Chinley, en route to Buxton in February 2017. (Ian Hardman)

No.45690 pilots No. 45407 (masquerading as No. 45154 *The Glasgow Highlander*) through New Mills in March 2018. (Ian Hardman)

The LMS duo of Nos 45690 and 45407 approach New Mills Signal Box with the 'High Peak Explorer'. (Ian Hardman)

Royal Scot Class locomotive No. 46115 *Scots Guardsman* crosses the Ribblehead Viaduct with the 'Dalesman Railtour'. (Ian Hardman)

No. 46115 *Scots Guardsman* working her final railtour in 2017; she is seen exiting Blea Moor Tunnel before being withdrawn for her ten-yearly overhaul. (Ian Hardman)

Scots Guardsman at Appleby station. A memorial stone commemorates the life of the 'Railway Bishop', Eric Treacy, who died here in 1978. (Ian Hardman)

Scenes of the sixties as 45690 *Leander* passes Maude Foster and a selection of vintage vehicles at Chinley in 2015. (Ian Hardman)

The old and the new cross Stockport Viaduct: over fifty years separates *Leander*, of 1936, and the Class 323, which was built in 1992 and is an example of the last class to leave Hunslet Engine Co. of Leeds. (Ian Hardman)

Leander exits Stockport, hauling 'The East Yorkshireman' in 2016. (Ian Hardman)

It is almost a time warp at Hebden Bridge, with very little giving away the year. *Galatea* approaches on a private tour to Bradford. (Ian Hardman)

A rare beast indeed – steam at Bradford Interchange. *Galatea* runs round her train at Bradford in 2017. (Ian Hardman)

On her inaugural railtour, *Leander* takes water at Brighouse on the 'Hadrian'. (Ian Hardman)

Standing in for the failed Bulleid Pacific *British India Line*, *Galatea* heads the 'Lune River Trust' special into Leeds. (Ian Hardman)

LMS 8F No. 48151 simmers opposite the former LNWR warehouse at Huddersfield. (Ian Hardman)

After a forty-year absence, BR Standard No. 76084 is seen powering up Wilpshire Bank at Vicarage Lane. (Ian Hardman)

No. 76084 approaches Pleasington in the full summer sun on its main line test run. (Ian Hardman)

A4 Pacific No. 60009 *Union of South Africa* pauses at Manchester Victorian en route for Bury in winter 2017. (Ian Hardman)

No. 60009 approaches Langho on test following boiler work in 2017. (Ian Hardman)

LMS Black Five No. 45231 is seen on test at Hellifield before changing hands from Bert Hitchen to her new owners, Icons of Steam. (Ian Hardman)

Hogwarts Castle, alias GWR No. 5972 *Olton Hall,* takes water at Hellifield before returning to shed at Carnforth. (Ian Hardman)

Black Five No. 45407 *The Lancashire Fusilier* is pictured en route to Bury with sister engine No. 44871 as the pilot. (Ian Hardman)

Driver Mick Kelley awaits the signal at Manchester Victoria with A3 Pacific No. 60103 *Flying Scotsman* on a light engine move to Bury. (Ian Hardman)

Bulleid Pacific No. 35018 *British India Line* exits Wilpshire Tunnel on a test run back to Carnforth, still wearing plain black livery. (Ian Hardman)

LMS 'Coronation' No. 46233 Duchess of Sutherland on the approach to Bamber Bridge with the outbound leg of the Cumbrian Mountain Express (Ian Hardman)

Timetabled main line steam returned during the 'Plandampf' over the S&C from 14 to 15 February 2017. Over 5,500 passengers were carried. Peppercorn A1 Pacific *Tornado* speeds toward Dent on 15 February 2017.

Running tender first, *Tornado* pilots Class 67 No. 67029 over the Ribblehead Viaduct.

Above and below: Awaiting her next departure, *Tornado* simmers at Skipton while passengers board the next train to Appleby.

Tornado and No. 67029 power toward Skipton.

Amid spectacular mountain scenery, *Tornado* crosses Dentdale Viaduct en route to Appleby.

Drifting steam signals the approach of *Tornado* as she rounds the curve into Dent – the highest station in England.